CELEBRATING HOLIDAYS

Memorial Day

by Rachel Grack

BELLWETHER MEDIA • MINNEAPOLIS, MN

Note to Librarians, Teachers, and Parents:

Blastoff! Readers are carefully developed by literacy experts and combine standards-based content with developmentally appropriate text.

Level 1 provides the most support through repetition of high-frequency words, light text, predictable sentence patterns, and strong visual support.

Level 2 offers early readers a bit more challenge through varied simple sentences, increased text load, and less repetition of high-frequency words.

Level 3 advances early-fluent readers toward fluency through increased text and concept load, less reliance on visuals, longer sentences, and more literary language.

Level 4 builds reading stamina by providing more text per page, increased use of punctuation, greater variation in sentence patterns, and increasingly challenging vocabulary.

Level 5 encourages children to move from "learning to read" to "reading to learn" by providing even more text, varied writing styles, and less familiar topics.

Whichever book is right for your reader, Blastoff! Readers are the perfect books to build confidence and encourage a love of reading that will last a lifetime!

This edition first published in 2018 by Bellwether Media, Inc.

No part of this publication may be reproduced in whole or in part without written permission of the publisher. For information regarding permission, write to Bellwether Media, Inc., Attention: Permissions Department, 5357 Penn Avenue South, Minneapolis, MN 55419.

Library of Congress Cataloging-in-Publication Data

Names: Koestler-Grack, Rachel A., 1973- author.
Title: Memorial Day / by Rachel Grack.
Description: Minneapolis, MN : Bellwether Media, Inc., 2018. | Series:
    Blastoff! Readers: Celebrating Holidays | Includes bibliographical
    references and index. | Audience: Grades K-3. | Audience: Ages 5-8.
Identifiers: LCCN 2017029517 | ISBN 9781626177536 (hardcover : alk. paper) |
    ISBN 9781681034584 (ebook)
Subjects: LCSH: Memorial Day–Juvenile literature.
Classification: LCC E642 .K68 2018 | DDC 394.262–dc23
LC record available at https://lccn.loc.gov/2017029517

Editor: Paige V. Polinsky   Designer: Tamara JM Peterson

Printed in the United States of America, North Mankato, MN.

Table of Contents

Memorial Day Is Here!

Families gather at the cemetery. They lay flowers on **military** graves.

bugler playing taps

A **bugler** plays **taps** while people stand quietly. It is Memorial Day.

Memorial Day honors **fallen soldiers** of the United States.

6

People remember their **sacrifice**. For many, it also marks the start of summer.

Who Celebrates Memorial Day?

People in the United States celebrate Memorial Day.

Memorial Day celebration in France

Other countries may also honor U.S. troops who died on their land.

Memorial Day Beginnings

Memorial Day began in Waterloo, New York, in 1866.

New York

N
W E
S

New York

Waterloo

Civil War battle

It honored those who died in the **Civil War**. The holiday was called Decoration Day.

Decoration Day, 1899

Decoration Day was celebrated every May 30th for many years. People later began remembering all fallen soldiers on this day.

It was renamed
Memorial Day
in 1967.

Time to Celebrate

Memorial Day now
falls on the last
Monday in May.

Schools close to respect **veterans**.
Many businesses also close for this
important day.

People decorate military graves with flags and flowers. American flags fly at **half-staff** until noon.

Many people take
a moment of silence
at 3:00 p.m.

Some buy red cloth **poppies** on this day. They wear the flowers to remember lives lost in service. The sales help veterans.

Make a Tissue Paper Poppy

Carry your poppy on Memorial Day to honor fallen soldiers.

What You Need:
- 1 black, 1 red sheet of tissue paper
- pencil
- 1 small, round lid or cup, for tracing
- 1 big, round lid or cup, for tracing
- scissors
- 1 green pipe cleaner

What You Do:
1. Trace three circles using the small lid or cup on the black paper. Cut out the circles and stack them.
2. Repeat step 1 with the big lid and red paper.
3. Center the black circles on top of the red circles.
4. Carefully poke the pipe cleaner through the center of the circles, pushing up from the bottom. Push through until about 1 inch of the pipe cleaner is poking up.
5. Bend the tip in half to make a hook shape in the center of the flower.
6. Hold the flower by the stem. Use your fingers to scrunch the tissue paper up. Fluff it out until the pipe cleaner tip is hidden in the black center.

2

4

People gather to celebrate freedom on Memorial Day. Some grill food or go to the beach.

Families watch soldiers march in parades. They remember those who died for the United States!

Glossary

bugler—someone who plays a bugle; a bugle is an instrument similar to a trumpet.

Civil War—the U.S. war between the Union, or northern states, and the Confederacy, or southern states, fought between 1861 and 1865

fallen soldiers—soldiers who died in military service

half-staff—about halfway down the flagpole; flags are flown half-staff to show respect for someone who has died.

military—the armed forces

poppies—bright red or orange flowers

sacrifice—something given up

taps—the song played at military funerals and at night to signal bedtime

veterans—those who served in the armed forces

To Learn More

AT THE LIBRARY

Cella, Clara. *Memorial Day*. Mankato, Minn.:
Capstone Press, 2013.

DeRubertis, Barbara. *Let's Celebrate Memorial Day*.
New York, N.Y.: The Kane Press, 2016.

Walsh, Barbara Elizabeth. *The Poppy Lady:
Moina Belle Michael and Her Tribute to Veterans*.
Honesdale, Penn.: Calkins Creek, 2012.

ON THE WEB
Learning more about
Memorial Day is as easy
as 1, 2, 3.

1. Go to www.factsurfer.com.

2. Enter "Memorial Day" into the search box.

3. Click the "Surf" button and you will see a
   list of related web sites.

With factsurfer.com, finding more information
is just a click away.

Index

The images in this book are reproduced through the courtesy of: PEPPERSMINT, front cover, pp. 16-17; U.S. Navy photo by Mass Communication Specialist 2nd Class Jennifer L. Jaqua/ Wikipedia, pp. 4-5; Yobro10, p. 4; Dorti, pp. 6-7; kali9, p. 7; fstop123, p. 8; njaj, pp. 8-9; Everett Historical, p. 11; Niday Picture Library/ Alamy, pp. 12-13; Dan Thornberg, p. 13; Hang Dinh, p. 14; a katz, pp. 14-15; glenda, p. 17; Monkey Business Images, p. 18; Tamara JM Peterson/ Bellwether Media, p. 19 (all); cdrin, pp. 20-21; Brent Hofacker, p. 20; studioarz, p. 22.